Contents

Lessons

Resources

Basic Card

Snowman Family

card front

card inside

HOLIDAY GREETINGS

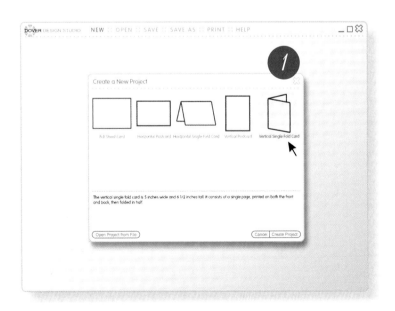

Helpful Hint!

Full instructions on how to use the software program can be found on the accompanying DVD.

1 Select the vertical card format.

2 Select the Snowman Family
image (IM001).

3 Enlarge the Snowman Family image
so it fills the card as shown creating a narrow
white border.

4 Print the card on an 8½"x11" sheet of white
cardstock.

5 For the inside of the card, use the forward
and back arrows to select side 3 of the card.

6 Type your greeting. We used the
Copperplate font in 18-point size.

7 Turn the cardstock over and reinsert it
into the printer. Print the inside.

8 Cut out your card using the crop marks as a
guide. Score in the center and fold in half.

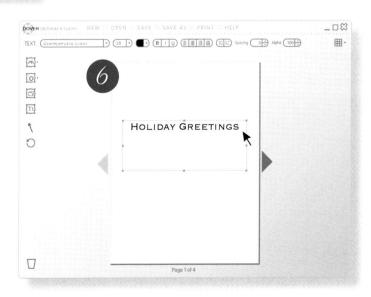

Basic Card Variations

card front

Happy Holidays Photo Card

◆ Use the horizontal card format and place your 6"x5" photo on the card, leaving a white border that is wider at the bottom.

◆ Type your greeting below the photo, slightly to the right of center. We used Certificate Script in 26-point size.

◆ Print the card on an 8½"x11" white cardstock.

Inside:

Go to side 3. Select and place the green holly image (IM002) just left of center. Type your message. Turn the cardstock over and print the inside of your card. Cut out using the crop marks, score in the middle and fold.

Embellishment:

Cut a ⅜" wide green grosgrain ribbon to 6½" long. Insert a gold mini brad in each end. Glue along edge of photo. Tie a shoestring bow and glue it as shown. Place gold swirls & flourishes stickers at the corners as shown.

card inside

Believe Card

card front

card inside

◆ Use the vertical card format. Select the Believe Santa image (IM003) and center it on the card. Use the gridlines as a guide to make the image 2½"x 3½" tall.

◆ Print on 8½"x11" sheet of white cardstock.

Inside:

Go to side 3. Select the Happy Holidays image (IM004) and center it on the card. Turn the cardstock over and print the inside of your card. Cut out, score in the center and fold in half.

Embellishment:

Tie a bow from ½" wide purple crepe ribbon; glue to the front. Place red jewel stickers at the corners of both images.

Envelope:

Select the full sheet format. Print the envelope image (EV001) on a piece of purple paper. Cut and fold according to the directions on page 34. On a separate full sheet, print out the bells image (IM005) the size shown. Cut out and glue to the flap.

card front

card inside

New Year Card

♦ Use the vertical card format and fill the card space with the Angel image (IM006).
♦ Print on an 8½"x11" sheet of white cardstock.

Inside:

Go to side 3. Place the same angel image near the fold but make her 1½"x2". Place a black image (IM160) next to the angel as shown. Place a white image (IM161) on top but let some of the black show around the edge. Type your message using 24 point Freehand font. Turn the cardstock over and print the inside of your card. Cut out your card following the crop marks, score in the center and fold.

Embellishment:

On the full sheet format place the tag image (TG001) then print. Cut out the tag and punch a ¼" hole in the narrow end. Fold a 5" length of ½" wide cream crepe ribbon. Insert the fold into the hole. Insert the ends through the loop then glue the tag to the card front.

card front

card inside

Christmas Greetings

♦ Use the vertical card format.
♦ Select the Santa face image (IM007).
♦ Enlarge Santa's image so it fills the card as shown. Notice his hat and some holly are cut off at the top but the words still show on the card.
♦ Print the card on 8½"x11" white cardstock.

Inside:

Go to side 3. Select the second Santa image (IM008) and place centered on the card. It's 2⅞"x4". Using Copperplate font in 18 point size, type the message below Santa. Turn the cardstock over and print the inside of your card. Cut out, score in the center and fold.

Background Card

Health, Happiness & Hope

card front

card inside

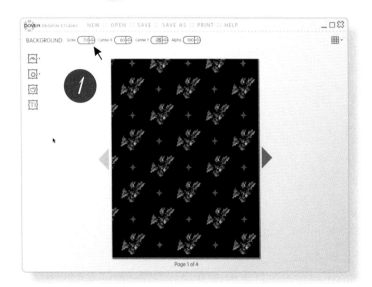

1 Open the vertical card format. Select the holly patterned background (PB001). Place it covering the entire card.

2 Select the red image (IM162). Place it centered on the card making a 2½"x4" red rectangle. Use the grids to help measure the rectangle.

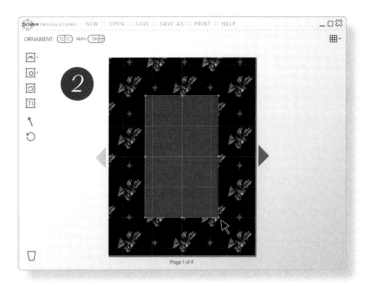

3 Select the "Wishing you…" artful greeting image (AG001) and place it over the red area.

4 Print on 8½"x11" white cardstock.

5 **For the inside:** Go to side 3. Place the smaller holly image (IM009) centered as shown on the finished card. Turn the cardstock over and print the inside of your card. Cut out following the crop marks. Score in the center and fold.

6 Open the full sheet format. Place a 4"x3" red image (IM162). Select the "From our Family…" artful greeting (AG002) and place on top. Print out the sheet. With scissors, cut around the scalloped edge of the greeting leaving a narrow red frame. Glue it as shown on page 6.

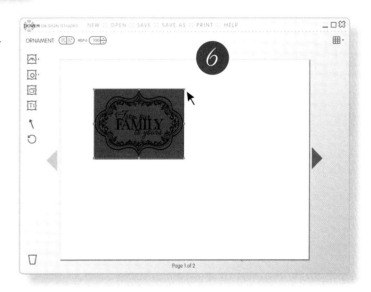

Background Variations

Fa La La La La *Two Patterned Backgrounds*

- Use the horizontal card format and place a red color (ED1D24) to fill the card.
- Select the button image (IM010) and place so ¾" of red shows on two sides.
- Choose the striped image (IM011) and position it as shown keeping it 2¼" tall. Print on 8½"x11" white cardstock.

Inside: Go to side 3. Place the narrow button image (IM012) along the top. Place the ⅛" tall red striped image (IM013) along the button bottom edge. Position the "La la la…" tag (TG002) on top. Turn the cardstock over and print the inside of your card. Cut out, score in the center and fold.

Embellishment: Use the full sheet format and place the caroling kids image (IM014) and the Fa La La circle tag (TG003). Print the sheet of white paper. Cut out the images. Glue ¼" wide green gingham ribbon above the red stripe and glue a bow as shown. Glue the kids in the center with the circle tag on the left. Glue buttons as shown. Fold a 1" ribbon in half and glue inside.

Joyous Angel *Two Diagonal Backgrounds*

- Use the full sheet format. Place the green angel patterned image (IM015) and a yellow angel patterned image (IM016). Print your white sheet and cut out the images. Cut the yellow angels diagonally in half.
- Use another full sheet format and place the Joyous angel image (IM017) and the clasped hands angel image (IM018).
- Position a 4"x3" green image (IM159) with a "May all…" artful greeting (AG003) on top. Print the sheet then cut out the pieces.

Front: Use a blank white 6½"x5" card and turn it with the fold at the top. Spread glue on half the card and place the green angel background paper as shown. Trim the excess paper. Repeat on the other half with the yellow angel background paper. Glue the Joyous angel in the center.

Inside: Cover half the inside with the yellow angel paper. Glue the angel and greeting overlapping as shown.

Embellishment: Wrap ¾" wide ivory sheer ribbon around the front flap and glue a ribbon bow as shown. Place gold crystals or gold jewel stickers on the trees and inside on the holly.

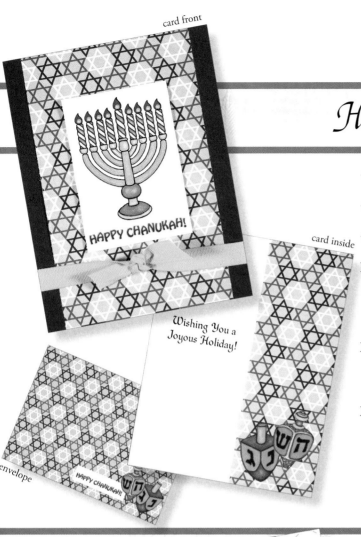

card front

card inside

Wishing You a Joyous Holiday!

envelope

HAPPY CHANUKAH!

Happy Chanukah *Two Vertical Backgrounds*

- Use the vertical card format and place the dark blue color (27416A) to cover the card.
- Place the Star of David image (IM019) so ⅜" of blue shows on each long side.
- Place the Chanukah image (IM020) in the center. Print on 8½"x11" white cardstock.

Inside: Go to side 3. Place the Star of David image along the right edge as shown. Type the greeting in 18 point Freehand font. Place two dreidel images (IM021 and IM022) as shown. Turn the cardstock over and print the inside of your card. Cut out, score in the center and fold.

Embellishment: Use an Xacto® pen knife to cut a ¾" long slit in the fold 1" from the bottom. Thread a ½" wide yellow grosgrain ribbon into the slit and wrap around the card front. Tie a knot and trim the ribbon tails.

Envelope: Select the full sheet format and place the envelope image (EV001). Print the sheet. Then place the gold Star of David patterned background (PB002). Turn the sheet over and print your envelope. Follow the cutting and folding directions on page 34 to make the envelope. Again select the full sheet format and place the Chanukah image (IM023) and two dreidels. Print the sheet then cut out the images. Glue on the front of the envelope.

Ho Ho Ho Santa *Cutaway Card*

card front

Let's be Merry & Bright

card inside

- Use the horizontal card format and place the diamond patterned background (PB003) to cover the card.
- Place the Santa image (IM024) as shown. Print on 8½"x11" white cardstock.

Inside: Go to side 3. Place the striped patterned background (PB004) to cover the card. Place a 4"x1½" red image (IM162) ½" from the top. Position the "Let's be…" artful greeting image (AG004) on top. Turn the cardstock over and print the inside of your card. Cut out, score in the center and fold.

Embellishment: Cut 1½" off the card front also cutting around the Santa image. Tie a knot in ½" wide red grosgrain ribbon and glue along the cut edge on the right. Glue more ribbon along the left edge. Inside the card, insert a swirl brad on each side of the greeting.

Frame Cards

Bringing You Christmas Cheer

envelope

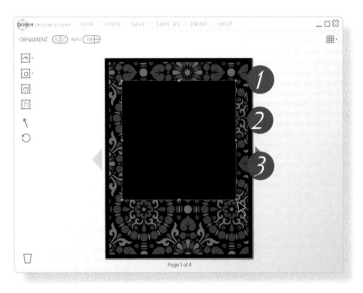

1 Use the vertical card format and place a black color (000000) to cover the card.

2 Select the red patterned image (IM025). Place it on the card, sizing it so some of the black color shows, forming a frame.

3 Select the black rectangle image (IM160) and place on the front of the card as shown.

4 Select the little girl image (IM026) and place her on top of the black area, allowing a black frame to show. Keep it the same width as the first black frame.

5 Again, select the black rectangle and center it below the girl; size it as shown. Place a white rectangle on top forming a narrow black frame.

6 Select the artful greeting (AG005) and place on top of the white area. Print the card on an 8½"x11" piece of white cardstock.

7 **For the inside:** Go to side 3. Select the black rectangle and place on the inside as shown. Select the red patterned image (IM027) and place on the black, creating a narrow black frame.

8 Place a smaller black rectangle in the center of the red patterned area. Place a white rectangle (IM161) on top forming a black frame. Place another artful greeting (AG006) over the white area. Turn the cardstock over and print the inside of your card. Cut out, score in the center and fold.

9 **Envelope:** Select the full sheet format. Print the envelope image (EV001) on red paper. Cut and fold following the directions on page 34. With another full sheet format place red print image (IM0025) twice, overlapping the images vertically so that the pattern matches Also place a 2½" black image with the little girl on top. Print and cut out both pieces, trimming the print image to 2½"x8". Spread glue over the envelope flap. Position the red print paper on top, turn the flap over and trim the red print to fit the flap. Glue the little girl image so the top half is on the flap. After inserting your card, glue the image down to seal the envelope.

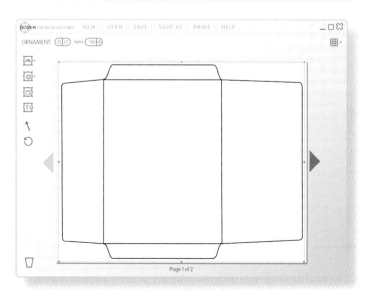

Frame Card Variations

card front

Have a Cozy Christmas Framed Photo Card

- Use the vertical card format and place a red color (D02729) to cover the card.
- Place a red/green plaid patterned image (IM028) inside the red, leaving a frame. Place a red rectangle (IM162), leaving two rows of plaid around it.
- Place your 3⅝"x5" photo inside the red leaving a narrow red frame.
- Print on an 8½"x11" piece of white cardstock.

Inside:

Go to side 3. Place a narrow plaid image (IM029) across the center of the card as shown. Turn the cardstock over and print the inside of your card. Cut out, score and fold.

Embellishment:

Use the full sheet format. Place both tags (TG004, TG005). Print and cut out. Tie a knot in a ¾" wide green ribbon and glue across the front as shown. Glue the smaller tag under the knot. Punch a ¼" hole in the top of the larger tag and tie more of the green ribbon as shown. Glue inside the card.

card inside

The Season's Greetings Offset Frame Card

card front

- Use the vertical card format and select the gold holly frame (IM030). Place it on the card front so there is a generous white frame around it.
- Select a black image (IM160) and place it even with the right edge of the card centered within the gold frame. It will measure about 3⅞"x4¾". Select a red image (IM162) and place it just inside the black.
- Place another black image inside the red allowing a generous red frame to show. Place the Christmas image (IM031) so there is a narrow black frame.
- Print on an 8½"x11" sheet of white cardstock.

Inside:

Go to side 3. Following the photo for placement and size, repeat the gold, black and red rectangles with the Christmas image. Type "Tidings of Joy" below the holly frame; we used 20-point Harrington font. Turn the cardstock over and print the inside of your card. Cut out, score and fold.

Embellishment:

Tie a bow in ¾" wide moss green ribbon and glue to the front. Inside the card: Fold a ½" long ribbon and glue next to the black frame.

card inside

12

card front

card inside

Think Snow Three Frames on a Cutaway Card

- ◆ Use the horizontal card format and place a navy blue color (283B5C) to fill the card.
- ◆ Place the blue dot image (IM032) leaving a blue frame. **Note:** The bottom area will be cut off to show the striped paper which is inside the card. Print on 8½"x11" white cardstock.

Inside:

Go to side 3. Place a narrow striped image (IM033) along the bottom edge. Place a 3¾"x1¾" blue dot image (IM037) in the center of the open area. Place a 2½"x 2¼" navy blue image (IM158) overlapping the dot. Place a white image (IM161) on top creating a narrow blue frame. Place the "Hoping this..." artful greeting (AG007) in the center. Turn the cardstock over and print the inside of your card. Cut out, score and fold. Cut off the front flap leaving an equal navy frame all around.

Embellishment:

Use the full sheet format. Place two navy blue 1¾" squares. Place a snowflake image (IM034 and IM035) on each one leaving a narrow navy frame. Place a 2" navy blue square with a "think snow" image (IM036) on top creating a slightly wider frame. Print and cut out. Insert a blue mini brad in the center of each snowflake then glue to the front. Place foam tape behind the mittens square and position it in the center.

Double Snowman Overlapping Frames

card front

card inside

- ◆ With the vertical card template, place a red color (D02729) covering the entire front.
- ◆ Select the green Happy Holidays image (IM038) and place it inside the red leaving a red frame.
- ◆ With the black image (IM160) place a 1⅞"x3½" rectangle on the right.
- ◆ Place a snowman image (IM040) inside leaving a narrow black frame. Repeat to place a black rectangle with another snowman image (IM039) overlapping on the left. Print on 8½"x11" white cardstock.

Inside:

Go to side 3. Place a 2" tall Happy Holidays image (IM132) at the top of the card. Place a black image as shown. Place a red image (IM162) inside leaving a black frame. Place the "Bringing you..." artful greeting (AG005) on top. Turn the cardstock over and print the inside of your card. Cut out, score and fold.

Embellishment:

Place gold holly outline stickers on each corner with red crystals or red jewel stickers over the holly berries. Inside, place a gold swirl outline sticker on each side of the greeting.

Window Cards

Believe in the Magic

card front

card inside

Believe...

in the magic of Christmas

1 Use the vertical card format and place a green color (12A34E) to cover the card. Place the white image (IM161) leaving a ⅛" green frame.

2 Place the blue image (IM156) leaving an even narrower white border. Use the grid to measure 1½" from the card top and place a 2¾"x3½" white image in the center (it will be the cut-out window). Position the Believe tag (TG006) in the corner as shown.

3 **Border:** Place a ¾" wide white image across the card staying within the blue area. Place the snowflake image (IM041) in the center creating a white frame. Print your card on 8½"x11" white cardstock.

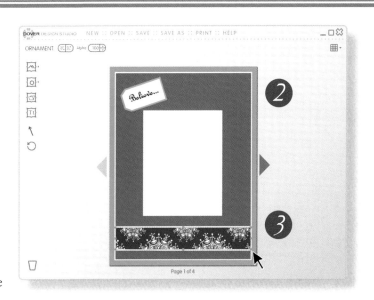

4 **Inside:** Go to side 3. Place a 3½"x4¼" green image (IM157) 1" from the top. Place the blue image inside creating a ¼" green frame. Position the 2¾"x3½" reindeer image (IM042) 1½" from the card top. For the sentiment, make a 3"x¾" green rectangle with a white image (IM161) on top forming a green frame. Type your message using 20 point TypoUpright font or use the tag (TG026). Turn the cardstock over and print the inside of your card. Cut out your card.

5 Place your card flat on a self-healing cutting mat or other surface. Use a ruler and Xacto® pen knife to cut along the white edge.

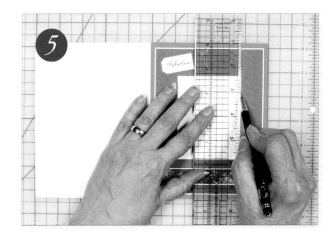

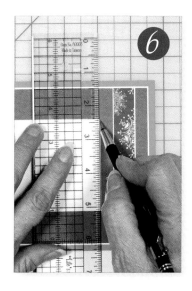

6 Turn your card and start at the corner to continue cutting out the white window. Be sure not to cut beyond the white edge. Repeat on each side of the window.

7 Remove the cut-out window. Score in the center of your card and fold. The reindeer image should show in the window. If not, you can go to the full sheet format and repeat the inside directions to make another inside image and greeting. Print on 8½"x11" white cardstock and cut out. Glue to the inside of your card aligning the pieces to show.

Window Card Variations

card front

card inside

Let it Snow A Framed Window

- ◆ Choose the vertical card format and place the lavender bordered image (PB005) covering the card.
- ◆ Place a 2¾"x3¼" lavender image (IM155) 1" from the top of the card.
- ◆ Place a white image (IM161) leaving a ¼" lavender frame.
- ◆ Position the "Let it snow!" tag (TG007) on the corner. Print your card on 8½"x11" white cardstock.

Inside: Go to side 2, Place the striped patterned background (PB018) to cover the card. Place a 3¼"x4½" lavender image ½" from the card top. Put the snowman image (IM043) on top leaving a ¼" lavender frame. Position the "Sending…" tag (TG008) overlapping the frame as shown. Turn your cardstock over and print the inside of your card. Cut out, score and fold.

Window: Following steps 5–7 on page 15, cut out the white window.

Embellishment: Tie a knot in ½" wide lavender dot ribbon. Trim the tails to 1" long and glue to the corner of the window. Fold a ½" length of dot ribbon and glue next to the inside tag.

'Tis the Season *Offset Window Card Using Metallic Gold Paper*

card front

- ◆ Use the full sheet format. Place a 5"x4¼" red/white striped image (IM044). Place a 1½"x3½" white image (IM161) on top ½" from the left edge.
- ◆ Place a 3⅛"x4¼" red image (IM162) with the Santa image (IM045) on top leaving a ⅛" red frame.
- ◆ Print on 8½"x11" white sheet. Cut out the pieces.
- ◆ Glue gold paper to cover the front of an 6½"x5" white card. Glue the striped rectangle ¼" from the fold. Cut out the white window following steps 5–7 on page 15.

Tags: Use the full sheet format and place the "'Tis the season…" tag(TG009) and the "Bringing..." tag (TG010). Print on gold paper. Cut out each tag.

Embellishment: Glue each tag to red paper and cut out leaving a narrow red frame. Glue the "'Tis.." tag to the front. Tie a bow out of ½" red grosgrain ribbon and glue on top of the tag.

Inside: Cut a 6½"x1" gold strip. Glue across the inside, 1½" from the fold. Glue red ribbon on top and trim the excess. Glue the Santa image so he shows inside the window. Add red crystals or red jewel stickers on each tag, on Santa's belt and the tip of his hat.

card inside

card front

card inside

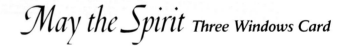

Merry & Bright Cutaway Frame Card

- ♦ Select the vertical card format and place a dark green color (4D8944) to cover the card.
- ♦ Place a 4"x6¼" lime green image (IM153) on top leaving a ⅛" dark green frame on three sides. Later, ¾" of the green front will be cut off as shown.
- ♦ Place a 3"x3¼" red image (IM162) ⅝" from the top. Place a white image (IM161) in the center leaving a ¼" red frame.
- ♦ Place the "Merry…" tag (TG011) as shown. Print on 8½"x11" white cardstock.

Inside & Front: Go to side 3. Place the striped patterned background (PB007) to fill the card. Turn the cardstock over and print the inside of your card. Follow steps 5–7 on page 15 to cut out the window. Score in the center and fold. Cut ¾" off the right front panel.

Embellishment: Glue red mini rick rack on the front and insert a gold star brad as shown. Select the full sheet format. Place a 3½" square green image (IM154) with a 3" square red image on top. Then position a 2¾" square green image with the reindeer image (IM046) on top. Place the "Sending…" tag (TG012) on the page. Print the sheet and cut out both pieces. Glue inside as shown.

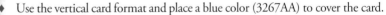

card front

card inside

envelope

May the Spirit Three Windows Card

- ♦ Use the vertical card format and place a blue color (3267AA) to cover the card.
- ♦ Place a 1½"x5¼" red image (IM162) ½" from the top and ⅛" from the right edge.
- ♦ Position three 1¼"x1½" white images (IM161) so each has a red frame. Print on 8½"x11" white cardstock. Cut out the card, score in the middle then fold.

Print: Use the full sheet format. Place the following: 1½"x5¼" red image, three images (IM047, IM048 and IM049), 2½"x3¼" red image with "May the spirit…" artful greeting (AG008) on top. Place a 1½"x2¼" red image and use 36 point Colchester Black font for the word "And." Make another text box and use 26 point Copperplate for the rest of the sentiment. Place a 1½"x1⅝" red image with the "open on…" image (IM050) on top leaving a narrow red frame. Print the sheet and cut out the pieces.

Card Front: Glue a 1"x6½" green cardstock 1¼" from the fold. Glue a ¾"x6½" gold paper in the center. Glue the "May the spirit…" greeting onto gold paper and cut leaving a ¹⁄₁₆" gold border. Glue as shown. Cut out the windows following steps 5–7 on page 15. Tie a bow with ½" green grosgrain ribbon and glue as shown.

Inside: Glue the red rectangle onto gold paper and cut leaving a ¹⁄₁₆" gold frame. Position with the images on top so they will show through the windows then glue in place. Glue the greeting to gold paper and cut leaving a ¼" frame. Then glue to blue cardstock and cut with a ⅛" frame. Fold the ribbon and glue behind the top. Glue the message as shown.

Envelope: Use the full sheet format. Place the envelope image (EV001) and print on the back of a gold paper. Cut out and fold following the directions on page 34. Glue a ¾" wide green cardstock over the edge of the bottom flap; trim the excess. Glue the top of the "open on" image to the flap and seal when the card is inside.

S-fold Cards

Bell-Ringing Santa

card front

open card

1 **For the card inside:** Use the vertical card format and go to side 3. Place the striped patterned background (PB017) to fill the card. Place a 3¼"x3⅞" white image (IM161) 1¼" from the top. Position a red image (IM162) creating a ¹⁄₁₆" white frame. Place a green image (IM154) leaving a ⅛" red frame on three sides and a wider frame on the bottom. Place the Santa with kids image (IM051) creating a ¹⁄₁₆" green frame. Position the "In the magic…" tag (TG014) at the corner. Print on 8½"x11" white cardstock. Cut out the card, score in the middle and fold.

2 Use the full sheet format and place a 2½"x6½" red image with the blue dot image (IM130) on top creating a ¹⁄₁₆" red frame. For the card focal, place a 3¼"x4½" red image with a 2⅞"x3⅝"green image in the center and a bell-ringing Santa image (IM052) on top forming a narrow green frame. Separately, place the "Believe" tag (TG013). Print the white sheet and cut out the three images; however, leave a ¹⁄₁₆" white frame around Santa's red frame.

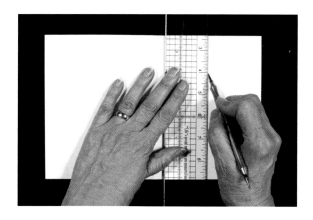

3 Unfold your card and place it flat on the table with the card front facing you (it will be white). Use a pencil to lightly mark a vertical line 2½" from the left. Use a ruler and stylus to score along the line. You can also use a ruler and the unsharpened, dull side of an Xacto® pen knife. Close the card.

4 Bring the right edge of the card front to the fold creating an S-fold card. Firmly press on the fold—a bone folder really helps. When you stand up the card, you'll see the S shape.

5 Glue the dotted paper over the card front.

6 Position the bell-ringing Santa on the front so it covers the inside Santa with kids image. Glue only the left side of the ringing Santa to the card front. Glue the Believe tag as shown. Tie a knot in ½" wide lime green grosgrain ribbon and glue under the Santa image. Place silver border stickers along both Santa images as shown. Place a silver crystal or silver jewel sticker at the end of each tag.

"S" Card Variations

Ho Ho Ho *Two Vertical Greetings*

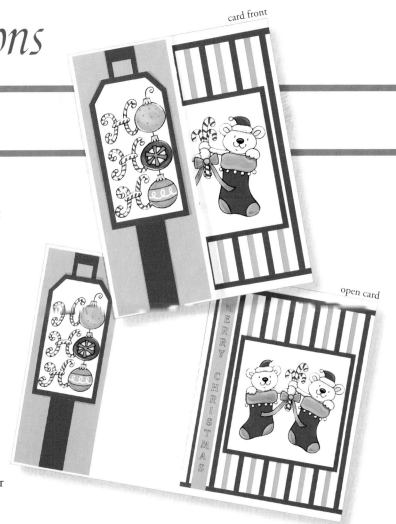

card front

open card

Card Inside: Go to side 3. Place a red image (IM162) so ¼" of white shows at the top and bottom. Position the red/green stripe (IM053) allowing ⅛" of red to show at the top and bottom. Place a ½" wide lime green image (IM153) ⅜" from the left edge—notice it stops at the edge of the red borders. Use 22 point Romana Outline font to write Merry Christmas. Place a 3½" red square in the center of the card. Position the bears image (IM054) creating a ⅜" red frame. Print your card on white cardstock. Cut out, score and fold.

Card Front: Use the full sheet format and place a 2¼"x6¼" lime green rectangle with a ¾" wide red rectangle in the center. In the center of the red area, place a ½" square of lime green ¼" from the red top. Place the Ho Ho Ho tag (TG015) over the lime green square as shown. Print out your sheet and cut out the green rectangle.

S-fold: Follow steps 3–4 on page 19 to create your S-fold card. Glue the Ho Ho Ho rectangle to the front of your card.

Christmas Puppy *Shaped S-Fold Front*

card front

card inside

Card Inside: Go to side 3. Place a lime green color (B1C050) to fill the card. Place a 2"x6" red plaid image (IM056) ¼" from the right side. Place a 2½"x3¼" red image (IM162) ⅞" from the left then centered top and bottom. Position a white image (IM161) creating a ⅛" red frame. Place the "Hoping Santa…" artful greeting (AG009) in the center. Print on 8½"x11" white cardstock. Cut out your card, score and fold.

Card Front: Use the full sheet format and place a 2½"x6½" red plaid image (IM056) with a 2"x6" lime green rectangle (IM153) in the center. Place a 4½" tall puppy image (IM057) so the left half is on the green rectangle as shown. Print out the white sheet. Cut out the image, trimming along the right side of the puppy.

S-Fold: Follow steps 3–4 on page 19 to create the S-fold card. Glue the rectangle to the card front allowing the puppy to cover the inside sentiment. Insert four silver brads as shown.

card front

card inside

Cheerful Penguins 3-Image, Stairstep Front

Card Inside: Go to side 3. Place a light blue color (B9CBF1) to fill the card. Position a 2½"x6½" blue snowflake image (IM058) at the left and a ⅝"x6½" image (IM059) on the right, ⅛" from the right edge. Place a 2¼"x2" medium blue image (IM150) overlapping the snowflakes by 1⅛" as shown. Place a light blue image (IM151) creating a very narrow medium blue frame. Place a 1¾"x1½" medium blue rectangle in the center with a white rectangle (IM161) creating a ¹⁄₁₆" blue frame. Position the "Christmas tidings…" artful greeting (AG010) in the center. Print on 8½"x11" white cardstock. Cut out, score and fold.

Card Front: Use the full sheet format and place a 2½"x6½" snowflake image. Place three 2" light blue squares with medium blue squares on top creating ¹⁄₁₆" light blue frames. Place a penguin image (IM060, IM061, IM062) on each square allowing a narrow medium blue frame to show. Also place the "Happy Holidays" tag (TG016). Print the white sheet and cut out the five pieces.

S-Fold: Follow steps 3–4 on page 19 to create your S-fold card. Glue the snowflake rectangle to the card front. Position each penguin square as shown making sure the middle penguin conceals the inside message; glue in place. Glue the tag as shown. Insert a pewter mini brad in the end of the tag. Tie a bow in ¾" wide sheer blue ribbon and glue as shown.

card front

card inside

envelope

Polar Bear with Gifts Color Blocked Card

Card Inside: Go to side 3. Place a light blue color (B9CBF1) to fill the card. Place a 2½"x3½" red image (IM162) on the right, ¼" from the bottom of the card. Position the polar bear image (IM065) creating a ¼" red frame on three sides. Place a 1¾"x2¼" red rectangle above the bear with a lime green image (IM153) creating a ¹⁄₁₆" red frame. Position the "May the Love…" artful greeting (AG011) on top. Place a 2¼"x2½" red rectangle as shown. Position the polar bear image (IM064) forming a red top and bottom border. Print on 8½"x11" white cardstock. Cut out, score and fold.

Card Front: Use the full sheet format and place a 2½"x6½" red rectangle. Place a 2¼"x6½" lime green rectangle (IM153) on the right side. Place the 2¼"x4¾" polar bear image (IM063) ⅞" below the top and flush with the right side. Place a ¼" wide red rectangle above the bear image. Place a 1"x5½" lime green rectangle. Then place a 2¾" square light blue image (IM151) with another polar bear image (IM066) on top creating a blue frame. Print your white sheet of paper. Cut out the images.

S-Fold: Follow steps 3–4 on page 19 to create your S-fold card. Glue the polar bear rectangle to the your card front. Tie a knot in ¼" wide red gingham ribbon and trim the tails to 1" long. Glue under the front bear image. Tie a bow with the ribbon and glue inside near the fold as shown.

Envelope: Use the full sheet format and place the envelope image (EV001). Print on the back of a red sheet of paper. Cut and fold following the directions on page 34. Glue the green strip to the front of the envelope 1" from the left side and glue the bear on top.

Flap Cards

Christmas Present

card front

card inside

1 Use the vertical card format and go to side 3. Place the brick color (A42027) on the inside of the card. Print on 8½"x11" white cardstock. Cut out the card, score in the middle and fold.

2 Use the full sheet format and place a 2¾" square Compliments image (IM067). Also place a 3½"x4½" brown image (IM149) with the girl image (IM068) on top creating a ⅛" brown frame. Print your white sheet and cut out both images.

3 Glue each image to a sheet of gold metallic paper. Cut out leaving a ¼" gold frame around the girl and a ⅛" gold frame around the Compliments image.

4 Glue the girl image centered on the front of the card, touching the fold.

5 Cut the card front trimming along the gold frame, removing the excess white card.

6 Glue the Compliments image inside the card so the flap hides it when the card is closed.

Flap Card Variations

Merry Christmas Santa *Right Side Flap*

- Use the vertical card format and place the plaid patterned background (PB008) to cover the card front. Place a 2⅝"x3¼" white image (IM161) ¾" from the right side and centered on the top and bottom.
- Place a sage green image (IM148) creating a narrow white frame. Position the "It was always…" artful greeting (AG012) leaving a narrow green frame. Print on 8½"x11" white cardstock.

Inside: Go to side 3. Place a 4"x6½" sage green image along the right edge. Place a 1" wide plaid image (IM069) along the fold. Position the 3"x1⅜" "A warm and…" artful greeting (AG013) at the bottom of the green area, as shown. Place a 3"x4" black image (IM160) above the greeting. Position the Santa image (IM071) creating a very narrow black frame. Turn the cardstock over and print the inside of your card. Cut out, score and fold.

Flap: Use the vertical card format and place a 4"x4¾" sage green image on the right side. Position a black image creating a ⅛" green frame. Place the Santa image (IM070) forming a very narrow black frame. Print on 8½"x11" white cardstock. Cut out the green frame **PLUS** add a 1" wide white piece on the right side. The 1" piece will hold the flap to the card. Score along the white flap and glue it to the back of your card. Fold the flap on top of the card front.

Embellishment: Tie a bow in ¾" wide sage green crepe ribbon and glue to the flap. Fold a 1" length of ribbon and glue at the top of the artful greeting on the front. Knot the ribbon, trim the tails to 1" and glue inside your card.

Christmas Children *With a Ribbon Closure*

- Use the vertical card format and fill the card with ivory color (FAEDD3). Place the ornament image (IM072) creating a ⅛" ivory frame.
- Place a 2¼"x4⅛" dark green image (IM147) ½" from the right side of the card and centered on the top and bottom.
- Position the little girl image (IM073) creating a ¹⁄₁₆" green frame. Print on 8½"x11" white cardstock.

Inside: Go to side 3. Fill the inside with the ornament patterned background (PB009). Turn the cardstock over and print the inside of your card.

Embellishment and Flap: Use the full sheet format. Place a 4½"x5" dark green image. Position the "Heartfelt…" artful greeting (AG014) in the center. Place a 3⅛"x5" dark green image with another little girl image (IM074) forming a ⅛" green frame. Print your white sheet and cut out the heart with a ⅛" green frame. Glue inside the card. Cut along the little girl's green frame **PLUS** add a 1" wide white piece on the right side. The 1" piece will hold the flap to the card. Score along the white flap and glue it to the back of your card. The little girl will fold on top of the card and hide the second girl image. Glue an 8" length of ⅝" green sheer ribbon behind the flap and another behind the left side of the card. Tie a bow to close the card.

card front flap

Christmas Greetings

card inside

Christmas Greetings

Ho Ho Ho

Snowglobe The Fold is on the Bottom!

♦ Use the vertical card format. Turn the snowglobe image (IM075) on its side and place in the center of the card, along the left side. Print on 8½"x11" white cardstock.

Card Inside: Go to side 3. Place a light blue color (B4D3FB) to fill the inside card. Place the striped patterned image (IM076) creating a ¼" frame on three sides. Place the snowglobe shaped image (IM077) turned so it is next to the left side. Position the tag (TG017) angled at the top as shown. Turn the cardstock over and print the inside of your card. Cut out, score in the center and fold.

Flap (the card front): Cut along the edge of the snowglobe creating a flap.

Embellishment: Tie a knot in ½" wide light green grosgrain ribbon. Trim the tails to 1½" long and glue them behind the card placing the knot touching the tag.

card front flap

card inside

envelope

Santa's Greetings Scalloped Flap

♦ Use the vertical card format and place a brown color (462F26) covering the card. Place a 4"x5" red snowflake image (IM078) in the center of the card.

♦ Place a 3½"x4¾" red image (IM152) in the center of the card front. Position a light brown image (IM145) creating a ⅛" red frame.

♦ Place the Santa image (IM079) so there is a ¼" brown frame. Print on 8½"x11" white cardstock.

Inside: Go to side 3. Place a 3½"x4¾" brown image (IM146) ⅝" from the top of the card. Position the red snowflake image (IM080) creating a ¼" brown frame. Turn the cardstock over and print the inside of your card. Cut out, score and fold.

Embellishment and Flap: Use the full sheet format and place a 2½"x2" red image. Position the "Have a Merry…" artful greeting (AG015) on top. Print your white sheet and cut out the greeting. Glue inside the card. Cut a 5"x3" red cardstock. Use scallop-edged scissors to trim one 5" side. Score 1" from the opposite 5" side. Fold along the score. Glue this red flap behind the top of the card so the scalloped edge folds down on the card. Wrap ⅛" brown grosgrain ribbon twice around the flap and tie a bow.

Envelope: Use the full sheet format and place the envelope image (EV001). Print on the back of a red sheet of paper. Cut and fold following the directions on page 34 but do not glue it closed. Use the full sheet format and place a 7½"x5" red snowflake image (IM081). Print the white sheet. Cut out the image.

To line the inside: Spread glue inside the envelope and press the snowflake image as shown. Cut off the excess image and glue your envelope together.

3-D Cards

Compliments of the Season

card front

card inside

1 Use the vertical card format and cover the card with the green patterned background (PB016). Place the angel image (IM082) in the center, 1" from the right edge. Place the Compliments image (IM083) below her. Print on 8½"x11" white cardstock.

2 **For the Inside:** Go to side 3 and place a narrow green patterned image (IM129) along the top of the card. Position a 2½"x1¾" dark green image (IM147) overlapping the green patterned area. Place a cream image (IM140) forming a narrow green frame. Position the "Wishing you…" artful greeting (AG016) to fill the cream area. Turn the cardstock over and print the inside of your card. Cut out the card, score in the middle and fold.

3 Use the full sheet format. Place another angel image and a 2"x7" words image (IM128). Print the white sheet. Cut out the images. Tear the right edge of the words image and glue the image along the fold. Trim any excess words paper.

4 Roll the torn edge to create more dimension.

5 Place foam tape on the back of the angel. Glue her over the angel on the card.

Helpful Hint!

When mailing a 3-D card, place a piece of cardstock on top of the front and slip into the envelope. With the extra padding, the card will pass through the mail machinery more easily.

3-D Card Variations

Happy Snowman *Multiple 3-D Pieces*

card front

- Use the horizontal card format and place the red dot patterned background (PB015) to cover the card front. Place a 2¼"x4½" white image (IM161) ⅜" from the right side and centered on the top and bottom. Place a striped image (IM125) creating a narrow white frame.
- Place a 4"x3¾" white image ½" from the left and overlapping the first rectangle. Position the berry image (IM126) forming a narrow white frame.
- Place a 2¾"x3¼" red image (IM162) 1¼" from the left edge. Place the happy snowman image (IM084) on top making a narrow red frame. Print on 8½"x11" white cardstock.

Inside: Go to side 3. Place a 2¼"x5" red dot image (IM127) next to the left edge. Turn the cardstock over and print the inside of your card. Cut out, score and fold.

3-D: Use the full sheet format and place the Let it Snow tag (TG018), another happy snowman image, the "Wishing you…" tag (TG019) and a snowman head image (IM111). Print the full white sheet. Cut out the hat and tie from the happy snowman image, the green tags and the hat from the snowman's head image. Punch a ⅛" hole in the tag.

Embellishment: Glue white rick rack along the card front as shown. Glue the tag 1¾" from the fold and tie a bow from ½" red grosgrain ribbon. Glue above the tag. Place foam tape behind the hat and the tie then place on the card front.

Inside: Glue white rick rack ½" from the left edge. Thread ⅛" red ribbon through the tag and glue as shown. Foam tape the cut-out hat onto his head.

card inside

Happy Penguin *Pearls Add More Dimension*

- Use the horizontal card format and fill the card with the dotted patterned background (PB010). Place a 2½"x2¼" green image (IM147) 1" from the top and even with the right edge.
- Place a red image (IM162) forming a ⅛" green top and bottom border. Type your greeting using 20 point Adastra Black font.
- Place a 3½"x4½" white image (IM161) overlapping as shown. Position a green image forming a narrow white frame. Place a red image creating a ⅛" green frame.
- Place the penguin image (IM085) making a narrow red frame. Print on 8½"x11" white cardstock.

card front

Inside: Go to side 3. Place a 1¼" tall dotted image (IM086) along the bottom edge. Place a 2¾"x4½" red image ¼" from the left edge. Place a green image creating a ⅛" red frame. Position the tree/birds image (IM087) forming a narrow green frame. Turn the cardstock over and print the inside of your card. Cut out, score in the center and fold.

card inside

3-D: Use the full sheet format. Place three penguin images and print the white sheet. Cut out these pieces as shown and foam tape them on the penguin. Place 3mm and 5mm white pearls on the wreath and hat. Tie a bow out of ¼" white metallic ribbon and glue under the greeting.

3-D pieces

card front

card inside

envelope

Christmas Cheer *Layered Paper Images and Glitter*

♦ Use the horizontal card format. Place the red patterned background (PB006) to cover the card. Place a 5¾"x3¾" black image (IM160) as shown.

♦ Position the Christmas Cheer image (IM088) creating a ⅛" black frame. Print on 8½"x11" white cardstock.

Inside: Go to side 3. Place the 3" tall red patterned image (IM124) ½" from the top of the card. Place a 3¼"x1⅞" black image in the center. Position the "Season's Greetings" artful greeting (AG017) on top creating a ⅛" black frame. Turn the cardstock over and print the inside of your card. Cut out, score in the center and fold.

3-D: Use the full sheet format and place two holly images (IM089). Place the holly image (IM090) and the white tag (TG020) with your message in 36 point Commercial Script. Print the white sheet. Cut out both images and place foam tape on the backs. Position at the corner of the front and inside images as shown.

Embellishment: Squeeze red glitter glue over the holly berries; let dry. Insert red embroidery floss into three ½" white buttons and knot. Glue two on the front and one inside. Rub a black ink pad along the edges of the card front.

Envelope: Use the full sheet format and place the red patterned background. Print your white sheet. Turn the sheet over, place the envelope image (EV001) and print the envelope. Following the directions on page 34, cut and fold the envelope. Punch a ¼" hole in the cut out tag and insert a ¼" black ribbon with stitching. Ink the edges black and glue to the envelope. Foam tape the holly and add red glitter glue over the berries; let dry.

card front

card inside

December 25 *Silk Flowers, Brads and a Button*

♦ Use the vertical card format and place a green color (224235) covering the card. Place a music note image (IM094) making a ¼" green frame.

♦ Place a 2¾"x4⅛" red image (IM143) ¾" from the left side. Position the little boy image (IM090) creating a ⅛" red frame. Print on 8½"x11" white cardstock.

Inside: Go to side 3. Place a 3" tall music note image (IM095) ¾" from the bottom of the card. Turn the cardstock over and print the inside of your card. Cut out, score and fold.

Embellishment: Use the full sheet format and place a 2"x2½" red image. Position the "Wishing you…" artful greeting (AG018) on top. Place the holly image (IM092) and the book image (IM093). Print your white sheet and cut out the images. Glue the artful greeting 1" from the fold. Put foam tape on the back of the book and holly images then place as shown. Insert silver mini brads into the silk poinsettias and glue to the front. Insert and tie white embroidery floss into a ¾" green button then glue as shown. Tie a knot in ½" red grosgrain ribbon and glue across one corner.

Even More Ideas

Santa & Friend *A Flap Card*

card flap

card front

card inside

- Use the vertical card format and fill the card with blue color (67ACD1). Place a red image (IM143) creating a ⅜" blue frame.
- Place a lime green image (IM153) making a narrow red frame. Print on 8½"x11" white cardstock.

Inside: Go to side 3. Place a 3¼"x4" blue image (IM142) in the center. Position a lime green image creating a ⅛" blue frame. Place a 2⅝"x3" red image leaving a ⅝" lime border at the bottom. Place the bird image (IM096) making a narrow red frame. Write your message using 40 point Colchester Black font in the wide lime border. Turn the cardstock over and print the inside of your card. Cut out, score and fold.

Flap: Use the full sheet format and place a 4⅝"x1¾" blue image. Place a red 1" square image ¼" from the left. Position a lime green square image creating a narrow red frame. Using 80 point Colchester Black font, type the letter M. In a separate text box type "erry" in 40 point font. Repeat to create a C block and type the rest of Christmas. Also place a 2¾"x4⅛" red image with the Santa & Friend image (IM097) creating a narrow red frame. Print out the white sheet. Cut out the blue flap **PLUS** 1" more on the right side. Score along the white edge and glue the white to the back of the card so the blue folds onto the front. Cut out the Santa image, place on gold metallic paper and cut creating a ⅛" gold frame. Glue to the card as shown.

Embellishment: Tie a bow in a ½" green crepe ribbon. Glue next to Santa's image and tuck the blue flap under the ribbon tails.

Santa's Elves *5" Square Card with 4 Front Images*

card front

card inside

- Use the horizontal card format and place the red color (D02729) to cover the card front.
- Place a 4¾" square dotted image (IM098) creating a ⅛" red frame on the top, bottom and left side (the rest of the red will be cut off to make the card 5" square).
- Position a 4" square red image (IM162) in the center of the dot.
- Place four elf images (IM099, IM100, IM101, and IM102) creating a narrow red frame around each one. Print on 8½"x11" white cardstock.

Inside: Go to side 3. Place a 2" square red image ½" from the top and 1½" from the left edge. Position the Star Elf (IM103) making a ⅛" red frame. Place a 3½"x1⅝" red image centered ¼" below the elf. Position a green image (IM141) creating a narrow red frame. Place the "Wishing you..." artful greeting (AG019) in the center. Turn the cardstock over and print the inside of your card. Cut the card so it is 5" square, score in the center and fold.

Embellishment: Place green and red crystals or jewel stickers on the front and inside as shown.

card front

card inside

Decorate & Celebrate *Diamond Window Card*

- ♦ Use the horizontal card format and fill the card with the tan color (D4B888). Place a holly image (IM104) along the left edge and another holly (IM105) on the right edge.
- ♦ Position the Decorate tag (TG021) on the left. Place a ¼" wide dark red image (IM143) in the center. Place a 2⅜" square dark red image (IM143) with a 2" square white image (IM161) in the center. Turn each square on point and place ¼" from the top. Print on 8½"x11" white cardstock.

Inside: Go to side 3. Place a dark red color (9F0005) to fill the card. Place a ½"x6½" green image (IM147) ½" from the bottom. Position the "Celebrate…" tag (TG022) ¼" from the right edge. Place the 4" tall green framed tree image (IM106) centered at the top. Turn the cardstock over and print the inside of your card. Cut out, score in the center and fold.

Window: Follow the cutting directions 5–7 on page 15 to cut out the white window.

Embellishment: Tie a bow out of ½" green grosgrain ribbon and glue under the tag.

card front

card inside

Joy Angel *3-D Angel with Glitter and Pearly Accents*

- ♦ Use the vertical card format. Place the snowflake patterned background (PB011) to cover the card. Place a 4"x5½" white image (IM161) in the center.
- ♦ Position the Angel image (IM107) creating a narrow white frame. Print on 8½"x11" white cardstock.

Inside: Go to side 3. Place the blue color (67ACD1) to cover the card. Place a 4⅛"x5⅝" white image in the center. Position the snowflakes image (IM108) creating a narrow white frame. Place the "Making spirits…" artful greeting (AG020) as shown. Turn the cardstock over and print the inside of your card. Cut out, score in the center and fold.

3-D: Use the full sheet format and place the angel image again. Print the white sheet. Cut out the angel and place foam tape on her back. Place her on top of the first angel.

Embellishment: Squeeze gold glitter glue on the angel's halo, along the gold areas of her dress design, over the stars in her hair and necklace. Squeeze green glitter glue over the word JOY. Squeeze pearlized glue over the design on her wings. Let dry.

Even More Ideas

card front

Jingle Bells Metallic Gold Accents

♦ Use the vertical card format and place a red color (9F0005) covering the card. Print on 8½"x11" white cardstock.

Inside:

Go to side 3. Place a 2¾" tall red image (IM143) in the center of the card. Turn the cardstock over and print the inside of your card. Cut out, score and fold.

Embellishment:

Use the full sheet format and place a 4¼"x6⅛" green image (IM154) with the Jingle Bells image (IM109) creating a ⅛" green frame. Place the Skating Santa image (IM110) in the center making him 1½"x3". Separately place a ⅜"x2" red image, a 1½"x2¼" ivory image (IM140) with the Skating Santa on top. Also place a 3½"x1¼" green image with your message in 28 point Colchester Black font. Print your sheet and cut out the pieces. Glue the ⅜" red piece to the corner of the Jingle Bells. Glue the remaining pieces to metallic gold paper and cut each one creating a ⅛" gold frame. Glue the pieces as shown. Tie a bow in ½" green grosgrain ribbon and glue along the side.

card inside

Sliding Penguin A Gatefold Card

♦ Use the full sheet format and place a 5"x6½" black image (IM160). Place the blue snowflakes image (IM112) creating a ⅛" black top and bottom border.

♦ Separately, place a 3½"x4⅝" black image with a red image (IM143) creating a ⅛" black frame. Position the Sliding Penguin image (IM113) forming a narrow red frame.

♦ Type the red message using Kidprint font in 20 point. Print the white sheet and cut out the pieces.

♦ Use the full sheet format. Place a 5"x6½" light blue snowflakes image (IM114) with a 3½"x1¾" black image 1" from the top. Place a white image (IM161) creating a ⅛" black frame. Use Kidprint font in 20 point to type your message in red using (FF0000) color. Print the white sheet and cut out the image.

Gatefold Card:

Cut 10"x6½" white cardstock. Bring the left and right edges to meet in the center (see the drawing above). Glue the light blue snowflakes piece to cover the inside of the card. Cut the dark blue snowflakes/black image in half vertically. Glue each piece to a flap on the card front. Glue **ONLY** the left side of the Penguin image to the left flap.

Embellishment:

Overlap a ½" sheer white ribbon with a ¾" blue dotted sheer and tie a knot. Glue on the front. Fold a 1" length of blue dot ribbon and glue next to the inside message. Insert a silver snowflake brad at the corner.

card front

card inside

Santa & Season's Greetings
Metallic Paper & Gold Pearl Accents

♦ Use the horizontal card format. Place the plaid patterned background (PB012) to cover the card. Print on 8½"x11" white cardstock.

Inside:

Go to side 3. Place the 1¾" tall plaid image (IM115) along the bottom. Place a 3"x4" green image (IM147) ½" from the right. Position the Santa image (IM116) creating a narrow green frame. Turn the cardstock over and print the inside of your card. Cut out, score and fold.

Embellishment:

Use the full sheet format and place a 2⅞"x4" green image with the Santa/Toys image (IM117) creating a ⅛" green frame. Also place a 6½"x1½" red image (IM143) with the "Season's Greetings" artful greeting (AG021) ½" from the left edge. Then place a 3¼"x2" red image with the "Merry Christmas" artful greeting (AG022) on top. Print the white sheet and cut out the images. Glue each to metallic gold paper and cut creating gold frames the widths as shown. Glue the Season's Greeting to the center of the card front with the Santa/Toys image on the right. Place 3mm gold pearls along the gold borders. Inside, glue the Merry Christmas greeting overlapping Santa as shown.

And to All a Good Night *Flap Card*

♦ Use the vertical card format and place a dark green color (29321E) to fill the card. Place a 2¾"x6¼" light green image (IM159) ⅛" from the left edge.

♦ Position the Fireplace image (IM118) inside the light green area. Type the message using 24 point Grant Antique font as shown. Print on 8½"x11" white cardstock.

Inside:

Go to side 3 and place the green squares patterned background (PB013) to fill the card. Place the 2" rounded black image (IM119) toward the left side. Turn the cardstock over and print the inside of your card. Cut out, score and fold.

Flap & Embellishment:

Cut the card front creating the same-sized green frame all around. Tie a bow in a ⅛" red grosgrain ribbon and glue inside the card. Close the card and wrap ribbon around the card and tie a bow.

Envelopes

For Your 5"x6½" Cards

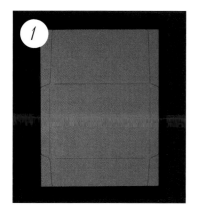

1 Use the full sheet format. Place the envelope image (EV001). Print your paper so the image will be on the inside of your envelope. In this photo, the red paper was double sided with red on both sides.

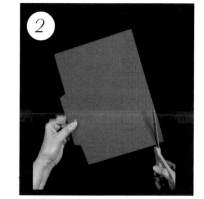

2 Cut out each corner following the lines.

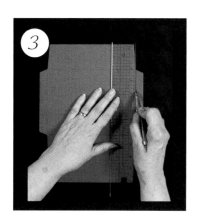

3 Score along each line using a ruler and stylus. This makes it easier to fold the envelope.

4 Position with the smaller flap at the top. Fold in each side. Press along the folds. A bone folder helps make crisp folds.

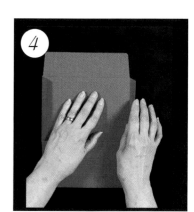

5 Fold the bottom flap up.

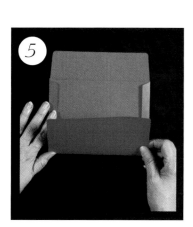

6 Fold the top flap down. Open the envelope and place glue over the side flaps and re-fold the bottom flap. Be careful not to put glue where the top flap will fold down. Embellish as you like!

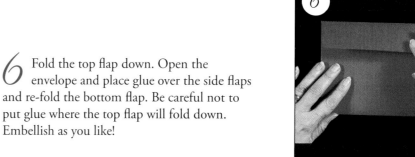

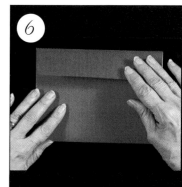

Print your sheet. You can use metallic papers, vellum or other light-weight specialty papers, too.

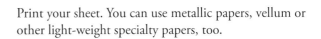

For a colored or patterned envelope:

Use the full sheet format and place a color or pattern to fill the sheet; then print. Use another full sheet format and place the envelope image (EV001). Turn your printed sheet over and print the envelope image on the back. **Tip:** To mail a patterned envelope, write the address on white paper, cut out and glue to the front.

Embellish the flap:

Glue cut out images to the flap or to the front of your envelope.

Embellish your envelope:

You can glue cut-out images to the front of your envelope. You can also use ribbons and cut-out images that are foam taped in place. These envelopes will be hand delivered or tucked inside a gift.

Line the envelope:

Follow steps 1–5 on page 34. Use the full sheet format and place a patterned background. Print the sheet and cut to 7¼" wide. Apply glue inside the envelope and on the top flap. Position a patterned background to cover the glue. Then press down. Turn the envelope over and trim the paper even with the flap. Follow step 6 on page 34.

Postcards

Postcards have a front and back. Be sure to leave ½ of the back for your address. These 6"x4¼" postcards are the largest that can be mailed at the postcard rate. You can have a vertical front yet a horizontal back!

card front

card back

Here Comes A Wish Postcard

Use the vertical postcard format and cover with a red color (9F0005). Place a 3¾"x5¾" green image (IM139) making a red frame as shown. Position the child image (IM120) creating a narrow green frame. Print on 8½"x11" white cardstock and cut out.

Back:

Use the full sheet format and place a 2⅞"x3¾" green image. Position a red image (IM143) creating a narrow green frame. Using the Copperplate font in 18 point, type your greeting. Place a 2½"x1" green image under the greeting. Position the houses image (IM121) forming a narrow green frame. Print the white sheet. Cut out the image and glue to the back of the postcard as shown.

Winking Santa Postcard

Use the vertical postcard format and cover with the Winking Santa image (IM122). Print on 8½"x11" white cardstock.

Back:

Go to side 2 and cover with the green color (4D8944). Turn the cardstock over and print the back of your postcard. Cut out your postcard.

Embellishment:

Use the full sheet format and place a 2¼"x3⅞" red image (IM143). Place a 2⅛"x3¾" green image (IM154) creating a narrow red frame. Place a 1¾"x3¼" red image making a wider green frame. Place the Coupon artful greeting (AG023) creating a narrow red frame. Print the white sheet and cut out the greeting. Glue to the back of your postcard.

card front

card back

card front

card back

Dancing Girls Postcard

Use the horizontal postcard format and cover with wreaths patterned background (PB014). Place a ⅝"x6" red image (IM143) across the center. Place the green tag (TG023) in the middle with the Dancing Girls image (IM133) as shown. Print on 8½"x11" white cardstock.

Back:

Go to side 2 and cover the left half with a red image (IM143). Position the smaller wreaths image (IM123) leaving a ⅝" red top and bottom border. Place the tag image (TG024) centered in the green area. Turn the cardstock over and print the back of your postcard. Cut out.

card front

card back

With Many Kindly Thoughts Postcard

Use the horizontal postcard format (don't worry, horizontal is correct) and cover with blue color (48718D). Place a ⅞" wide red image (IM162) 1¼" from the left side. Print the white sheet.

Back:

Go to side 2 and cover with yellow angels patterned background (PB019). Place a 2½"x3¾" blue image (IM138) ¼" from the left edge. Position A Merry Christmas Santa image (IM134) creating a narrow blue frame. Turn the cardstock over and print the back of your postcard. Cut it out.

For the front:

Use a full sheet format and place a 3½"x5⅜" red image. Place the words image (IM135) creating a narrow red frame. Print the white sheet. Cut out the words image and glue to metallic gold paper. Cut out creating a ⅛" gold frame. Glue to the front of your cardstock postcard.

card front

card back

Hi There! Postcard

Use the vertical postcard format and cover with lime green color (B0BF50). Place the holly frame image (IM136) as shown. Place a 3¼"x4¼" red image (IM162) with the Hi There! image (IM137) creating a narrow red frame. Print on 8½"x11" white cardstock.

Back:

Go to side 2 and cover with red color (CF2729). Place a lime green image (IM153) creating a ⅛" red frame. Place the 1½"x3¼" holly image (IM104) along the bottom and rotate the image as shown. This card will turn on its side. Place a ½"x4¼" red image (IM162) above the holly. Turn the cardstock over and print the back of your postcard. Cut it out.

Embellishment:

Use a full sheet format and place a 1⅜"x2¼" red image. Position a white image (IM161) making a narrow red frame. Place the "Wishing you…" artful greeting (AG001) creating a narrow white frame. Print the white sheet and cut out the greeting. Glue to the back of the postcard as shown.

Images

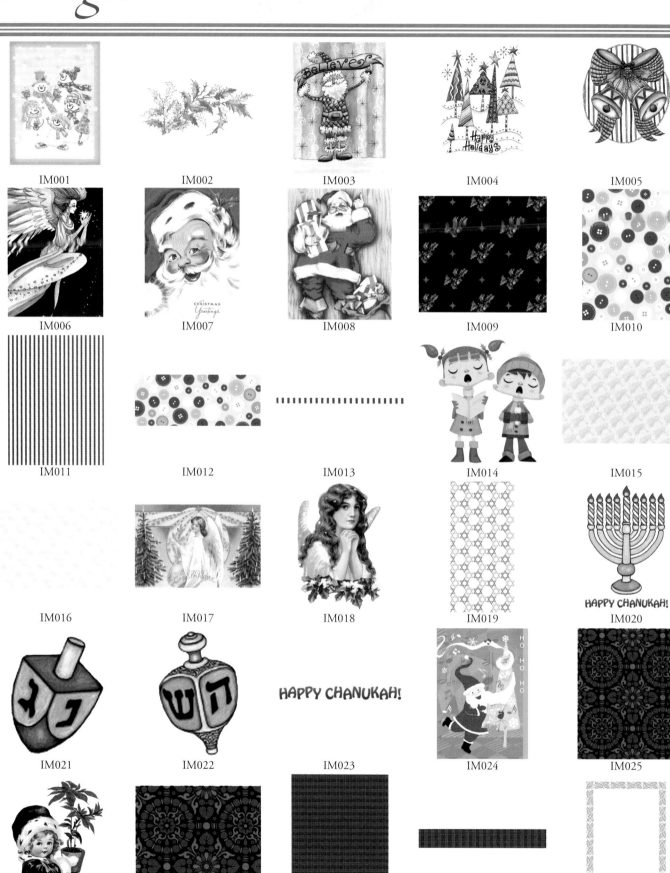

IM001

IM002

IM003

IM004

IM005

IM006

IM007

IM008

IM009

IM010

IM011

IM012

IM013

IM014

IM015

IM016

IM017

IM018

IM019

IM020

IM021

IM022

IM023

IM024

IM025

IM026

IM027

IM028

IM029

IM030

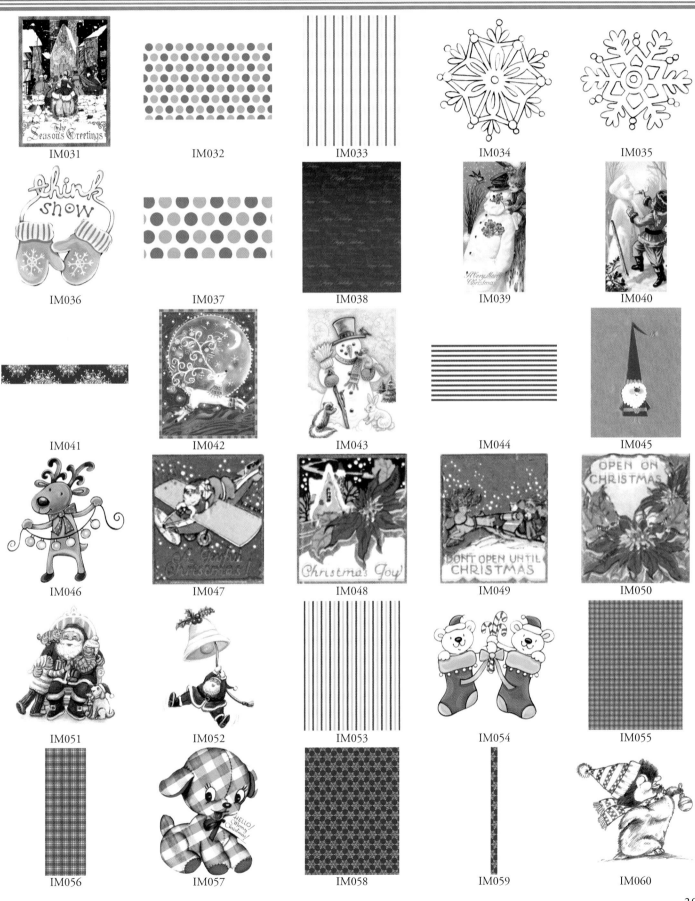

IM031

IM032

IM033

IM034

IM035

IM036

IM037

IM038

IM039

IM040

IM041

IM042

IM043

IM044

IM045

IM046

IM047

IM048

IM049

IM050

IM051

IM052

IM053

IM054

IM055

IM056

IM057

IM058

IM059

IM060

Images

IM061

IM062

IM063

IM064

IM065

IM066

IM067

IM068

IM069

IM070

IM071

IM072

IM073

IM074

IM075

IM076

IM077

IM078

IM079

IM080

IM081

IM082

IM083

IM084

IM085

IM086

IM087

IM088

IM089

IM090

IM091

IM092

IM093

IM094

IM095

IM096

IM097

IM098

IM099

IM100

IM101

IM102

IM103

IM104

IM105

IM106

IM107

IM108

IM109

IM110

IM111

IM112

IM113

IM114

IM115

IM116

IM117

IM118

IM119

IM120

Images

IM121

IM122

IM123

IM124

IM125

IM126

IM127

IM128

IM129

IM130

IM131

IM132

IM133

IM134

IM135

IM136

IM137

IM138

IM139

IM140

IM141

IM142

IM143

IM144

IM145

IM146

IM147

IM148

IM149

IM150

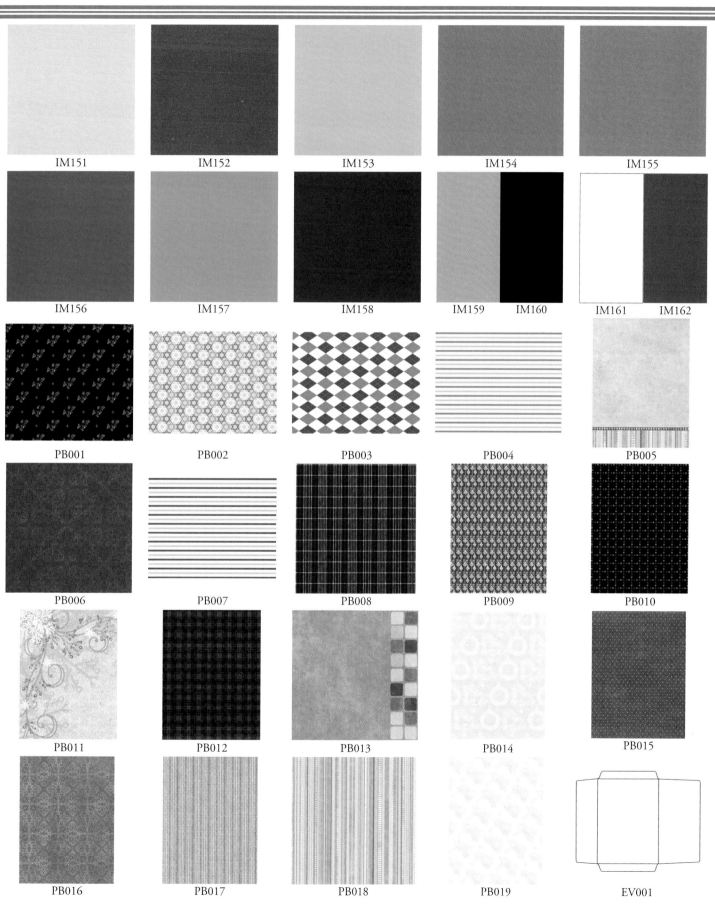

IM151 IM152 IM153 IM154 IM155

IM156 IM157 IM158 IM159 IM160 IM161 IM162

PB001 PB002 PB003 PB004 PB005

PB006 PB007 PB008 PB009 PB010

PB011 PB012 PB013 PB014 PB015

PB016 PB017 PB018 PB019 EV001

Artful Greetings

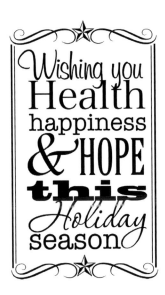

AG001

AG005

AG002

AG006

AG003

AG007

AG004

AG008

AG009

AG010

AG011

AG012

AG013

AG014

AG015

AG016

AG017

AG018

AG019

AG020

AG023

AG021

AG022

AG024

AG025

AG026

AG029

AG027

AG028

AG030

Tags

Wishing you a new year filled with happiness and joy

TG001

la la la la la
Tis the season to be jolly

TG002

Fa la la la la la

TG003

Have a cozy Christmas!

TG004

Wishing you warm and fuzzy feelings this season.

TG005

Believe...

TG006

Let it snow!

TG007

Sending you warm winter wishes

TG008

'Tis the season to be jolly

TG009

Bringing you holiday cheer

TG010

Merry and bright

TG011

Sending you Christmas Cheer

TG012

Believe

TG013

In the magic of Christmas

TG014

TG015

Happy Holidays!

TG016

Christmas Greetings

TG017

Let It Snow!

TG018

Wishing you a warm & cozy winter!

TG019

TG020

DECORATE & Celebrate

TG021

Celebrate THE SEASON

TG022

TG023

MAY YOUR CHRISTMAS BE BRIGHT AND HAPPY

TG024

TG025

in the magic of Christmas

TG026

TG027

TG028

TG029

TG030

TG031

TG032

TG033

TG034

TG035

TG036

TG037

TG038

TG039

TG040

TG041

TG042

TG043

TG044

TG045

Fonts

Adastra Black

A B C D E F G
H I J K L M
N O P Q R S T
U V W X Y Z

Freehand Normal

A B C D E F G
H I J K L M
N O P Q R S T
U V W X Y Z

Romana Outline

A B C D E F G
H I J K L M
N O P Q R S T
U V W X Y Z

Typo Upright

A B C D E F G
H I J K L M
N O P Q R S T
U V W X Y Z

Certificate Script

A B C D E F G
H I J K L M
N O P Q R S T
U V W X Y Z

Grant Antique

A B C D E F G
H I J K L M
N O P Q R S T
U V W X Y Z

Colchester Black

A B C D E F G
H I J K L M
N O P Q R S T
U V W X Y Z

Harrington Normal

A B C D E F G
H I J K L M
N O P Q R S T
U V W X Y Z

Commercial Script

A B C D E F G
H I J K L M
N O P Q R S T
U V W X Y Z

Kidprint Regular

A B C D E F G
H I J K L M
N O P Q R S T
U V W X Y Z

Supplies

Basic Supplies
ruler
pencil
stylus
paper trimmer and/or scissors
bone folder
self-healing cutting mat
retractable pick
Xacto® pen knife
white cardstock
white paper
glue stick or other paper adhesive

Happy Holidays Photo Card *(page 4)*
gold swirl stickers such as Swirls &
   Flourishes Dazzles™ stickers
⅜" wide green grosgrain ribbon
gold mini brads

Believe Card *(page 4)*
½" wide purple crepe ribbon
red crystals or red Jewel Dazzles™
   stickers

New Year Card *(page 5)*
½" wide cream crepe ribbon

Fa La La La La Card *(page 8)*
¼" wide green gingham ribbon
⅝" wide yellow button
½" wide red button

Joyous Angel *(page 8)*
gold crystals or gold Jewel Dazzles™
   stickers

Happy Chanukah *(page 9)*
½" wide yellow grosgrain ribbon

Ho Ho Ho Santa **(page 9)**
½" wide red grosgrain ribbon
green swirl brads

Have a Cozy Christmas *(page 12)*
¾" wide dark green crepe ribbon

The Season's Greeting *(page 12)*
¾" wide moss green crepe ribbon

Think Snow *(page 13)*
blue mini brads
foam tape

Double Snowman *(page 13)*
gold holly stickers such as Stacked
   Holly Dazzles™ stickers
red crystals or red Jewel Dazzles™
   stickers

Let it Snow *(page 16)*
½" wide lavender dotted grosgrain
   ribbon

Tis the Season *(page 16)*
½" wide red grosgrain ribbon
red crystals or red Jewel Dazzles™
   stickers
gold metallic paper

Merry & Bright *(page 17)*
red mini rick rack
gold star brad

May the Spirit *(page 17)*
¾" wide green grosgrain ribbon
gold metallic paper
blue and green cardstock

Bell-Ringing Santa *(page 18)*
½" wide lime green grosgrain ribbon

Christmas Puppy *(page 20)*
silver round brads

Cheerful Penguins *(page 21)*
¾" wide blue sheer ribbon
pewter mini brad

Polar Bear with Gifts *(page 21)*
¼" wide red gingham ribbon

Christmas Present *(page 22)*
gold metallic paper

Merry Christmas Santa *(page 24)*
¾" wide sage green crepe ribbon

Christmas Children *(page 24)*
⅝" wide dark green sheer ribbon

Snowglobe *(page 25)*
½" wide light green grosgrain ribbon

Santa's Greeting *(page 25)*
⅛" wide brown grosgrain ribbon
mini scallop scissors

Compliments of the Season *(page 26)*
foam tape

Happy Snowman *(page 28)*
white rick rack
½" wide red grosgrain ribbon
foam tape

Happy Penguin *(page 28)*
3mm & 5mm self-adhesive white pearls
¼" wide white metallic ribbon
foam tape

Christmas Cheer *(page 29)*
red glitter glue
red embroidery floss
cream buttons
¼" wide black with white stitched
   ribbon
foam tape

December 25 *(page 29)*
silver mini brads
red silk poinsettias
white embroidery floss or white thread
¾" wide green button
½" wide red grosgrain ribbon
foam tape

Santa & Friend *(page 30)*
½" wide light green crepe ribbon

Santa's Elves *(page 30)*
red crystals or red Jewel Dazzles™
   stickers
green crystals or green Jewel Dazzles™
   stickers

Decorate & Celebrate *(page 31)*
½" wide green grosgrain ribbon

Joy Angel *(page 31)*
gold glitter glue
green glitter glue
pearlized glue such as white pearl
   Stickles
foam tape

Jingle Bells *(page 32)*
metallic gold paper
½" wide green grosgrain ribbon

Sliding Penguin *(page 32)*
½" wide white sheer ribbon
¾" wide blue dotted sheer ribbon
silver snowflake brad

Santa & Season's Greetings *(page 33)*
metallic gold paper
3mm gold self-adhesive pearls

And to All a Good Night *(page 33)*
⅛" wide red grosgrain ribbon

With Many Kindly Thoughts *(page 37)*
metallic gold paper